BY THE SAME AUTHOR

Poetry

Adam's Thoughts in Winter

First Light & Other Poems

Criticism

Norman Cameron: His Life, Work, and Letters

Student Guide to George Orwell

Student Guide to Philip Larkin

Student Guide to Robert Frost

Student Guide to Seamus Heaney

The Shakespeare Controversy (with Kim Holston)

As Editor

A Movement of Minds:
Nine American Poets of the Late Nineteenth Century

Collected Poems and Selected Verse Translations
of Norman Cameron (with Jonathan Barker)

SELECTED AND NEW POEMS

'A Sketch of Warren Hope' (1983) by Tom Bostelle

SELECTED AND NEW POEMS

WARREN HOPE

Greenwich Exchange
London

Acknowledgments

Some of these poems originally appeared in the following periodicals: *Blue Unicorn, Chronicles, Cumberland Poetry Review, Dialogos, Drastic Measures, The Elixir, The Epigrammatist, Folio, The Formalist, Hellas, Light, Nebo, The New Compass, NewsArt, Poetry Durham, Pulpsmith, The Scotsman, The Schulkyll Valley Journal, The SHOp* (Ireland), and *The Smith*. In addition, a number of these poems appeared in several pamphlets and an anthology published by Robert L. Barth (Edgewood, Kentucky). Finally, some of these poems also appeared in a pamphlet published by The Scienter Press (Louisville, Kentucky). My thanks to the editors and publishers involved.

Greenwich Exchange, London

First published in Great Britain in 2020
All rights reserved

Selected and New Poems © Warren Hope, 2020

This book is sold subject to the conditions that it shall not, by way of trade or otherwise, be lent, resold, hired out or otherwise circulated without the publisher's prior consent in any form of binding or cover other than that in which it is published and without a similar condition including this condition being imposed
on the subsequent purchaser.

Printed and bound by imprintdigital.com
Cover design by December Publications
Tel: 07951511275

Greenwich Exchange website: www.greenex.co.uk

Cataloguing in Publication Data is available from the British Library

Cover art courtesy of Shutterstock

ISBN: 978-1-910996-47-8

for Jessica and Jason again

CONTENTS

Selected Poems

    A Citizen of Hap *15*

    The Only Prize *16*

    No Motley, No Armor *17*

    Artemis and Actaeon *18*

    Freedman to his Kin *19*

    An Unsuccessful Mission *20*

    Base Camp *21*

    Kilroy in Dalat *22*

    Reflections of a Returnee *23*

    Fall Expenditure *24*

    Better You Sleep *25*

    The Love of Summer *26*

    The Chandeliers *27*

    Generation to Generation *28*

    The Waiting Boat *30*

    A Hopeful Legacy *31*

    Change of Tenants *32*

    An Elegy for Raffety *33*

    Heraclitus's Other Life *36*

    The Reason for the Hours *37*

    History of a Great American Family Fortune *39*

    The Initiation *40*

    The Boarders *41*

    A Family Picnic *43*

    Adam's Thoughts in Winter *45*

Night's Mere Sonnid *46*

Beowulf's Funeral *47*

Apologia *48*

Victrola *49*

Owners and Occupants *50*

The Lawn Ornament *51*

On Akira Kurosawa *52*

A Private Anniversary *53*

The Unknown Trumpeter *55*

The Plot *56*

The Office Party *57*

The Arrest *58*

The Inner Circle *59*

The Sign *60*

Day's End *61*

A Case of Identification *62*

An Epistle from Barnabus *63*

Tu Fu Replies to a Query About Li Po *64*

The Condition *65*

The Master's Routine *66*

Things Change *67*

It's Time *68*

First Light *69*

Corporate History *70*

The Third Aspect *71*

Moving In *72*

The Way *73*

A Conclusion *74*

Deep Sleep *75*

The Promise *77*
The New Year's Gift *78*
On A Beach *79*
At Dawn *80*
General Giap in 2006 *81*
Point of No Return *82*
Yard Work *83*
Express *84*
Garlands *85*
A Lacquered Fan *86*
Translations *87*
Druthers *88*
Waking *89*
Inconsiderable *90*

New Poems

Old Snapshot of Office Life *93*
Reflections on a Cornish Fairy Tale *94*
A Friend of Camus Remembers *95*
The Spy Who Stayed Out in the Cold *96*
Two Horses *97*
The First Lady's Initiative *100*
On the Country Estate of Julius Martialis *101*
A Picture of Jerome *103*
A Portrait from the Life *105*
A Celebration *106*

SELECTED POEMS

A CITIZEN OF HAP

When I first washed up on the shore of hope
I did not say that anything but luck
Had led me here, a remnant of a wreck:
By birth I am a citizen of hap;
So do not show surprise when from that heap
I finally emerge with stiffened neck,
My strange clothes torn, with cracked lips that I lick,
Speaking an alien tongue from that of hope.

Know that my neck will smoothly move again,
My clothes will be your country's costly robes,
A new soft skin will blossom on my lips
With no tart memory of life on ships,
And when I, in your language, speak of hopes,
The sea that brought me here will make spring rain.

THE ONLY PRIZE

These two tall trees whose branches intertwine
Provide us with a shading canopy,
A respite from the traffic of exchange
(Trumped up demands supplied by shoddy goods),
The business deals closed by our busy crooks:
The sly handshakes, fake grins, and nasal lies
Performed as rites or charms to win a prize
By those who, from their birth, could never see
The only prize cannot be won or bought
But given, as when, beneath this canopy,
Made by these trees whose branches intertwine,
Your gentle fingers firmly lock in mine.

NO MOTLEY, NO ARMOR

Motley would suit me at an ancient court,
A time with space enough for jesting truths,
Though I think crowns should sit on museum shelves,
Giving our storytellers themes – like elves:
The blood lust of a regicide's descendant
Drags thoughts of headless kings across my brain.

No matter; I am faced with no such choice;
Laboring under a straight-faced, cowardly rule
There's little temptation to war or play the fool.
No motley, no armor, I court you with my voice.

ARTEMIS AND ACTAEON

My eager dogs ran shy, but much too late
To warn me that we'd crossed a boundary,
Had trespassed on a clear, unfenced estate
Where blindest luck had led me so I'd see

White Artemis, her arms down, streaming wet,
Who met me with no greeting, simply frowned,
Turning my dogs against me, in a sweat
To spill stag's blood upon the moon-soaked ground.

FREEDMAN TO HIS KIN

A house slave used to come out in the fields,
Talking against my master and his ways,
Saying field niggers burn out all their days
With no increase, save to the master's yields.
I told him, 'Look there at our shacks, bright shields
Against the rain and sun; and when wind plays
Among these blooms my head spins in a daze;
And hear those birds? Who cares who power wields?'

My mistress and her young ones surely cried
The day their daddy and my master died,
But that old houseboy wouldn't spend one tear,
Standing and staring there beside the bier;
Next day, he brought a whip out to the fields,
Scaring the birds while beating us for low yields.

AN UNSUCCESSFUL MISSION

All that remains of lurching from those hills
Where we had hovered for what seemed like hours,
Searching for remnants of a crew who crashed,
Is how the can of bread I'd saved was crushed
And that odd sense of panic – as when you're stuck
In traffic and you feel your car roll back
If other cars suddenly pull away.

What the crew's families buried, I can't say.

BASE CAMP

Watching, first, Woody Allen, then Jacques Cousteau,
We sit in monsoon mud charmed by a glow
That trickles technicolor on a tent.
Our nightly movies never cost a cent.

Friendly artillery fires a round.
                                      It's short.
The crowd, stampeding, rises with a snort.
One casualty resulted from this attack:
I saw a man with footprints up his back.

KILROY IN DALAT
for Bob Barth

The Chinese owner of that Swiss chalet,
A home converted to a restaurant,
Must have assumed that I would find it funny,
That I would merely laugh, as he had laughed,
To see that stuccoed wall of clumsy proofs,
The countless handprints and marks made by boots –
Vague remnants of a juvenile emotion.
But I surprised myself as much as him
When I took out a knife, cut off my patch,
And joined the ghostly scramble up that wall
To place my unit's emblem with the rest.

REFLECTIONS OF A RETURNEE

A sitting duck. Easy to recognize.
Though now the giveaway is not round eyes
So much as how I sit well back from doors
And wait to be the last to board a bus.

FALL EXPENDITURE

They're burning off their leaves across the road
Without a need for warmth or light,
At least no conscious need:
They simply wish to neatly spend their waste.

But see how men like moths are drawn by flame:
The man stays out to tend the fire
Unnecessarily,
And idle neighbors come to stand and gaze –

Savage attraction! This fall expenditure
Of brittle superfluities,
Attraction like the charm
Of dead words incandescent on a page.

BETTER YOU SLEEP

Better you do not know. Better you sleep.
Completely unaware of how I wake
And on one elbow watch your active lids,
The indecipherable semaphore of dream
Or nightmare. Better you do not know I hear
The angry grinding of your teeth, the speech
Of torment language hides. Better you sleep.
Better you do not see me as I move
This wayward strand of hair from your hawk nose.
Better you do not know. Embarrassment
Would never let me pull this gesture off
With so much grace before an audience.
Even the audience of you. Better you sleep
As I slide down to nuzzle your left breast
And nuzzle it until you (smiling) wake.

THE LOVE OF SUMMER

I've sought out summer and her lushness in
The most unlikely places imaginable
So often now – at four my little feet,
Squeaking in huge galoshes, led me straight
Into a snowdrift and clean out of sight –
I start to think what I've been after all
This time must be that darkness, that silence, that cold,
Myself there at the center, listening –
Not for the footsteps of salvation or
My own hysterical appeals for help
But to the way my regulated breath
Extends the love of summer to the snow.

THE CHANDELIERS

Revolving chandeliers of mirror-glass
Come back to me tonight from Saint Anne's Dance.
The odd effects they make: scattering light
As luminescent bugs that crawl up arms
And over faces, dance around the walls,
And gather on the ceiling in two crowns.

Father Murphy with his whiskey breath
Blusters again at shameless boys who smoke
'Without the decency or common sense
To go outside.' And fragile girls, with eyes,
Try once again to trap reflected light
Beneath their shoes, and laugh.
                                And sorrow comes.

Not the embarrassments of early love,
And not nostalgia for a golden age
Of trigonometry and radios,
But what that ceiling must have felt the night
Those chandeliers gave way in unison
With no one in the place to see their fall.

GENERATION TO GENERATION

I want to take my daughter by the hand,
Sit her beside me in my small red Ford,
And take her on a joyride through memory.

I'll show her where her great-grandmother lived
On Frankford Avenue near Shackamaxon Street –
A gold-star mother
Waging a cheerful war with creditors
And Jehovah's Witnesses;
I'll loiter with her on the marble steps
Of Sunday afternoons on Memphis Street,
And ask her to put her ear to earth
To hear my grandfather speak of Satchel Paige,
To hear my grandmother singing Men of Harlech;
I'll walk with her on Hagert Street
(Both of us, through familiarity,
Oblivious to the smells of Catties Galvanizing Works)
And point out my young self –
His buttocks pressed against a fireplug,
Gleefully spraying rainbows in the air;
We'll visit in the cramped and damp backyard
Of childhood,
Relishing kitchen smells and radios,
Climbing the Babel-like tower of lattice work,
Sailing the ocean on a glider bought at Sears;
I'll show her narrow streets, radiant with puberty –
Those crumbling steps beneath a rusty sign
That magically creaks if lovers are truly in love;
I'll sit with her, for hours, in Henry's Bar –
Drinking in New Year's Eves she never knew,

Laughing with mummers she will never know;
We'll walk in darkness beside the incessant river,
Filling the night with talk of the Wilson Line,
Of Riverview Beach and Soupy Island,
Of the park commemorating Penn's robbery of the
        Indians,
Of the sign which reads Philadelphia The Electric City –
With so many burned-out lightbulbs we'll lose count.

I'll drive her home, tuck her in bed,
Bend down to touch my lips to her smooth head,
Then watch her fragile nostrils pulse
The silent dream of love and death in sleep.

THE WAITING BOAT

It's not yet dawn
But I can see
My grandfather
Step from the light
Of a little house
In the Cornish village
Of Flushing.

I see him skid
On cobbled streets
Down to a pier
Where he unties
A waiting boat
Then rows across
Falmouth Harbor
To work.

I see him leaning
Back in a chair,
A Lucky burning
Between his lips,
Unaware
That, as he describes
This daily scene
From years ago,
My fingers curl
Around those oars.

A HOPEFUL LEGACY

I once held but a future interest in
The brown distinctive seals my father wore,
The folded vellum of my mother's skin,
The crinkled records of a nameless score:
My stature passed by statute with my grin
From smugglers and gunrunners to a bore
Who swayed young children from the life of sin,
Bequeathing me my deep, ancestral snore.
Now with my present interest, I work a chin
Remarkable for its narrowness, produce a store
Of repetitive anecdotes, and flex a thin
Wrist, moving spidery fingers; but at my core
I found a startling, hopeful legacy:
My father smiles through my daughter's eyes at me.

CHANGE OF TENANTS

Our red shag carpet and that mock-Tiffany globe
The former tenants used to hide the bulb
Gave the room a brothel-like effect,
Leaving me puzzled how to fix it up.
But when you walked in naked, with a gold
Bracelet clasped around your thin, left wrist,
Birds scattered with the sound of snapping twigs.

AN ELEGY FOR RAFFETY

> Of Frank W. Raffety we have not the honour to know anything, except what we have gathered from this little volume and from its title-page. But he must be a singularly interesting gentleman ... Sometimes Mr Raffety fairly takes our breath away, as when he informs us that Gray's tomb can be seen in the little churchyard of Stoke Pogis 'with the elegy written upon it'. Can Mr Raffety be acquainted with the length of the *Elegy* and with the proportions of a tombstone? ... 'There is,' says Mr Raffety, 'no more stirring lyric than "The Cotter's Saturday Night"', a remark that shows that Mr Raffety does not know what a lyric poem is. But to look for blunders in Mr Raffety's pages would be to look for leaves in a summer forest.
> – John Churton Collins in *Ephemera Critica* (1901)

But Collins couldn't know what it was like –
Heading out every morning after toast
And home each afternoon just after tea:
It wasn't easy being Raffety.

Sometimes he paused beside a dusty hedge,
Finding through leaves a web a spider wove
The night before. He loved the delicacy,
The iridescence, the cunning artistry –

But, sighing, moved along the road in pants
That glowed an iridescence from the seat,
That bagged a bit too much about the knee,
And bore the ink blots of his industry.

Seated before his class, he'd lose himself
In daydreams out the window as he'd done
When still a boy, then turn quite suddenly
And gently struggle for authority

Over the mocking faces of his charges.
He gently struggled, too, to keep inside
The words he feared he'd stammer urgently:
'Look lively to your futures – study me!'

Instead, he offered them concocted scraps
Of schoolbook lore he'd toyed with now for years:
'Today, lads, let's explore discovery.
Picture four tiny ships in 1493 ... '

At home, the evening dishes cleared away,
He entertained the wife and children with
Arias of operas he loved to parody,
'The Cotter's Saturday Night' as grand finale.

The silence when the children fell asleep
Drove him toward the window where he watched
Street lamps in fog as beacons out at sea
And whistled through pursed lips, unconsciously.

The missus spoke, then, of the grocer's bills,
The price of coal, the clothes the children wore,
Her knitting needles clicking steadily.
He took the pen up, nodding knowingly,

The papers in confusion on the table,
Turning over volume after volume,
Knocking together *Books Worth Reading, A Plea* ...
It wasn't easy being Raffety.

Collins, of course, was right. Old Raffety
Should not have taken up the pen, presumed.
But many do far worse with far less cause.
In memory of Frank W. Raffety: RIP.

HERACLITUS'S OTHER LIFE

He left his only book in the Temple of Artemis
Where he would lounge or pass the day at dice –
Taking his chances, you might say, with the Queen
Rather than joining the civic life of men;
And there's that rumored version of his death
That says he was attacked by baying hounds.
Like Actaeon.
              Beyond belief, I know,
But aren't his fragmentary works a track
Of bloody hoofprints left in virgin snow?

THE REASON FOR THE HOURS

How to explain the reason for the hours
Spent on my back – the tired eyes closed, the ears
Straining to hear the breathing of the house
As waves of dead men wash up on the brain?

Our neighbor, tending roses after rain –
His fingers twisting small blooms from a limb –
Says he still thanks the war for overtime
And laughs to learn I'm Johnny Appleseed.

The Indians behind the rose of Sharon,
Beyond the Alleghanies of our walk,
Accept with smiles the seeds I offer them
But do not seem too keen about the book.

Reverend Trout commits a Sunday sermon
Against the starched fronts of our long-sleeved shirts
This windless August morning, till Grandad,
Hearing a tugboat on the Delaware,

Declares it's quitting time and leads us out.
He tells the one about the minister
Who used a peppermint to time his talks
And ruined dinners with a button once.

After supper, against the cyclone fence,
Watching his red nose set behind a glass,
I rest my ear against a clump of earth,
Hoping to hear the hooves of my lost tribes,

But only catch, perhaps, the 39
Shuddering to a stop on Cumberland Street.
Someone returning from a funeral home
Steps from the trolley car, clicks up the block,

Brushes against the crepe hung on the door,
And though my brother says that no one should,
I cry as, swaying upstairs in thick arms,
A whisper tells me to go back to sleep.

HISTORY OF A GREAT AMERICAN FAMILY FORTUNE

Humble beginnings: a bottled water plant:
A joke, in fact, first dreamed up by an aunt
Who often drawled, 'Folks will buy anything',
And urged the family to have a fling.

They filled the bottles from the garden hose
And packed the crates themselves, wearing old clothes
Out in the garage on Sunday afternoons:
The aunt watched sales go up like loosed balloons.

But all those orders really forced her hand:
What else could she do except expand?
A personnel department, rented space,
Global distributorships ... then near disgrace:

Somebody started the rumor some customers died
And so the aunt, who never actually lied,
Named a grand-niece's husband president,
Pleased with the gravity of his 'No comment.'

THE INITIATION

The white enamel kitchen table where
The elders met in murmuring debate,
Hands folded solemnly as if in prayer
Or flitting high to make articulate
A sense their tongues couldn't wrest from air,
No longer shines as when, through bedroom grate
I peered, a silent witness, pressed an ear
Against the cool and liquid metal late
At night, somehow convinced my patient stare
And straining ear could bind me to the great,
Gain me admittance to the circle there,
Earn me the status of initiate.
But table, hands, and words – half-heard, half-seen –
Twitter away as cardinals from an evergreen.

THE BOARDERS

I once could count on them to stay upstairs.
At times the floorboards creaked beneath their weight
And made me wonder what they did all day –
Pictured thick clouds of smoke and rolling dice,
Shirt-sleeved discussions of the latest war,
Crossword puzzles, socks to rinse or mend,
All punctuated with long naps and tea.

Of course I welcomed them downstairs for meals.
They'd scamper deftly down two winding flights
And stand around the table awkwardly –
Their wool caps in their hands, their sheepish grins
Apologizing for being in the way,
Not sitting down until they had been asked.
But seated, they would eat the meal with relish –
Huge dripping slabs of ham with succotash,
Bowls of sweet potatoes, apple sauce,
Coffee cooled in saucers and slurped down,
And finally the plates wiped clean with bread.
All this without a word, then back upstairs.

The other night the house was full of guests,
Laughing and talking pleasantly enough,
When suddenly my eyes were drawn toward
The stairway. All three heads were bobbing there
Like hungry robins on a lawn in May
And though I strode toward them frowning they
Fluttered among the guests, turned music on,
And fixed gigantic drinks. They introduced
Themselves as near relations whom I had

Mistreated shamefully, cracked antique jokes,
Drew coins from people's ears, played songs on spoons,
And winked. Before I knew it they had pinched
The backside of each woman in the room,
Picked several pockets and as many fights,
And sent me open-mouthed to fetch the coats.

And yet I still remember that I laughed
So hard the tears came to my eyes as they
Stood grinning at the door, seeing out guests,
Before they took me with them up the stairs.

A FAMILY PICNIC

While I slept, my dead were gathering,
A little crowd around a redwood table,
Eating and talking in their canvas chairs.

The two grandfathers drag their chairs away
Into the lengthening shade, books on their laps,
To argue the Apocalypse again.

I'm sitting in between them, at their feet,
Smelling the rich cigars, listening to the words,
Reading their bony fingers as a text.

The aunts and uncles, in the twilight, tease
Each other with good-natured raillery,
Mild complaints concerning food and love.

I sit among them in my uniform,
Laughing and shaking my head, a constant no;
The girl beside me squeezes my arm yes.

My father's mother says it's time to go.
I lift her like a baby in my arms
And place her down beneath the flowerbed,

Caress her yellowed hair and kiss her cheek,
Circle her little plot, moaning and wailing,
My face held tightly in my trembling hands.

None of the others come to comfort me.
They mill around and look the other way,
Waiting for me to lift them, one by one,

And reunite them, gently, with the earth,
As they once carried me and kissed goodnight
When it was time for me to go to sleep.

ADAM'S THOUGHTS IN WINTER

Picking the fruit, a mindless entertainment,
Gave me an easy feeling of accomplishment.
The unresisting limbs. The smell. Enough
Sweetness and tenderness to drain the heart.
Another order of existence bred
In the small plot of vegetables. The row
Of radishes performed dramatically
Without much help from me. The carrots failed
No matter what I did – poor shrimpish things.
But when at night the squash grew luminous
I somehow thought that that was thanks to me.
All summer long Eve spoke about my loss
Of dignity, but then she smiled and bowed
To harvest that poor first crop with her hands.

NIGHT'S MERE SONNID

Long severing with my vogue sense of geld,
Lacking the where what all to grately earn,
Locking the wear wit tall to greatly love,
Fashioned to, with a little lick, come, leave,
End yet I've merried marry in her time:
Wince up in a tomb, by good begot,
Our hero here (O see ken you sigh)
Fell from a shucking appletrue to say
An apfelbit betwine his lapse and get
A legend pairodese, a starried tome
Causing the cwenly flood to love and lave,
Causing the kengly corn to leaf and love,
Replenishing by night wet die did burn:
At rainbough's bend there is a pate of guilt.

BEOWULF'S FUNERAL
(Lines 3169-3182 of Klaeber's *Beowulf*, 3rd edition)
Translated in memory of Abraham Bronson Feldman, 1914-1982

Around the mound the brave in battle rode,
The sons of noble sires, twelve in all.
They would lament their loss, cry for their king,
Utter a sorrowful song, speak of the man:
They praised his prowess and his work in war,
Deemed him most daring.
                 It is fit for man
To honor with his words his friendly lord,
To love him from the heart when he must go
Led from the body-home.
                 And so bemoaned
All of the people of the Geatish tribe,
Those hearth-companions mourned their dear lord's
    death:
They said of him that of all kings on earth
He was the mildest and most gentle man,
The kindest to his people and the most eager for fame.

APOLOGIA

Do not mistake my formal reticence
For mere distraction or rude arrogance:
I simply fear my shameless tongue will hint
How, like some whimpering beast, I hide when hurt.

VICTROLA

A footstool let me wind the aging crank
But someone had to lift me up to see
The round container filled with shiny needles
And the peculiar action of the arm.

I used to jut my hand and elbow out
In imitation of that metal arm
And then made revolutions on the rug
To bugle calls recorded by Pathé –

My first experience of martial strains:
Reveille; assembly; taps. The echo seemed
To mourn the gold stars hanging in the window,
Making them pendant from everybody's eyes.

Someone put on another record then.
The rug became a rich and fertile field
Where mares ate oats, and little lambs ate ivy,
And my dead stared through wreaths of their forced
    laughter.

OWNERS AND OCCUPANTS

They still are here. Despite the cans of paint,
The brushes, vacuum cleaner, scouring pads.
Despite our sofa, tables, chairs, and books.
Despite new drapes. The voices of our kids.
They still are here.
                    At first it seemed a game,
Laughing and picturing the people who
Painted the woodwork dreadful shades of grey,
Never replaced the bent venetian blinds,
And left old magazines and pins behind.

A tall, bow-legged man who stooped, perhaps,
Nodding at night beneath a burning lamp
As his short, chubby wife made tea, or read
The magazines, or loosed pins from her hair.

I saw them out beneath the trees in spring.
He cut the grass, she hoed a patch of yard,
Then they both sighed and rocked here on the porch.
Mildly eccentric. Kept to themselves, I'd say.
No sign of either animals or kids.

Whether they really lived this way or not,
They still are here. At first we welcomed them.
But now that their odd stains defy our efforts
And paper roses bleed through painted walls
We start to think we'll never feel at home.

THE LAWN ORNAMENT

I grace his hedge-enclosed exterior
By standing here in silence. As a guard,
Or as a household god: my blank regard
Blessing or cursing every visitor.
But that I'm neither guard nor god he knows:
I serve him as a colorful memory
Of gracious living under slavery:
'Here, hold my hoss, boy, mind you watch him close.'

In summer when the children play near me
I almost learn to love my livery,
And yet my services exact a price:
On snowy winter evenings, sheathed in ice,
I soon become my master – heavy, white,
Then flake and crumble through his dreams all night.

ON AKIRA KUROSAWA

This small boy, dressed up as an emperor,
Kicks fallen cherry blossoms up as snow:
He dreams himself a legendary robber
Who proved heroic when forced to play the ruler.

His eye records the workings-out of fate
Suggested by disguises that reveal:
The warrior as beggar at the gate
Or Faust within a petty bureaucrat.

Dissolve to Watanabe on a swing,
Singing a love song to the falling snow,
His dying voice somehow the murmuring
Of children playing on the grass in spring.

A PRIVATE ANNIVERSARY
In memory of the man who wrote under the name Max Nomad

They weren't left here by a party hack,
These long-stemmed roses strewn on Marx's grave:
I visualize a withered man, but brave,
Who rents a little box in Tooting Bec.

The box is lined with shelves for note and book:
A door placed on two files forms a desk
Where towering notecards shape an arabesque
Of crimes the bourgeois scholars overlook.

A window lets him glimpse crowds in the street.
He knows he does not love the cut-rate mass –
The long-haired boys with eyes like small dead fish,
The girls who'd think Class War's a punk-rock hit,

Much less their plodding parents, stupefied
By the state's crooked games of work and war,
By their own dreams of pleasure – gin, a whore –
Who cheer each time a savior's crucified.

And yet he would not serve the ruling class
For all their benefits and pension plans:
He was not born to clap on paper chains
And shuffle at the bidding of a boss.

He has become, perhaps, a class of one,
Maintaining solidarity with ghosts,
One of the lost, living among lost hosts
Who will not usher in a revolution –

And that, he can admit, is just as well:
'To think we might have bashed skulls and spilled blood,
Convinced the cause we served was just and good,
Only to make a replica of hell.'

Still, on this private anniversary
He takes the Underground to Camden Town,
Seeks out a florist's shop, and then walks on
Until he stands in Highgate Cemetery:

He does not say a word or make a move
And yet the moment is a celebration,
A kind of atheist's commemoration
Of what it means to have known faith and love:

A futile ritual, a silly act
By a crouched figure in a workman's cap:
A gentle creature in a grotesque trap
Who's kept the sense that life is sweet intact.

THE UNKNOWN TRUMPETER

> 'There is an unknown second trumpet man ... '
> from notes to a Louis Armstrong album

For all I know he spends his nights on grates
Clinging to clouds of steam,
Trying to sleep and, maybe, dream
Of when he traveled widely playing dates.

Or it could be he's been retired for years –
Tucked in a nursing home
Where a rare visitor will come
To speak to him and wonder at his tears.

But it seems much more likely he is dead,
A fading memory
Among old friends and family
That soon will fail to trouble any head.

No matter how he lives or how he died,
His life has one plain meaning,
The jubilation of his playing,
A joyousness that will not be denied –

A joyousness that brings joy to this room,
Making me offer thanks
To one who from the nameless ranks
Raises sweet riffs tinged with a sense of doom.

THE PLOT

Characters in stories I will never write
Meet weekly at the local library,
The members of a pallid little sect
Demanding they want equal rights with me.

The notices they put up on the board –
Illiterate, almost illegible –
So touched me I decided to attend
And thus support the truly negligible.

The femme fatale, addressed as Madam Chair,
Brings a petition forward for a vote.
The hoodlum grins. The spinster clears her throat.
I raise my hand, say 'aye', and disappear.

THE OFFICE PARTY

There's something sad about the way
That people, drawn together by
The need to earn their weekly pay,
Become a mimic family.
It happened once again today:
We formed a circle awkwardly
To celebrate a colleague's birthday
With store-bought cake and decaf tea.

Imagine with what shivering
We'd line this mourner's bench, the globe,
Bereft of even this thin robe:
No slice of cake, no cup of tea,
No off-key voices raised to sing
And fortify our frailty.

THE ARREST

He knocked his pipe out on the windowsill
And looked up at the clock. As always, noon
Or midnight – which one would not matter soon:
In this job there is always time to kill.
And yet the cases, once, gave him a thrill –
A bit, he thought, like translating a rune:
Skill, patience, luck, and something more. A boon?
Lucas came in then with the criminal.

'It's good of you to come ... Yes, I admit
The case against you is a little weak
But ... Hardly that, I wouldn't call it pique.
Say rather, if you like, the pieces fit.'
Going out he heard Lucas on the phone:
'Maigret at last arrested Simenon.'

THE INNER CIRCLE

Only the inner circle has the code:
Its members, to each other, are unknown.
Security has forced us down this road.
Only the inner circle has the code.
You must have faith if, when you lift the phone,
You listen closely to your own voice drone:
'Only the inner circle has the code:
Its members, to each other, are unknown.'

THE SIGN

That vacant warehouse with the rusty sign
Over its crumbling steps might not have been
The ideal place to go to be alone;
And we did not believe the legend of
The sign's ability to tell true love;
And yet we both agreed that when it creaked
We knew our lives had suddenly been changed.

DAY'S END

It is the day's end that becomes you most.
I wouldn't criticize the face you put
On for the world each morning, any more
Than I'd oppose the rising of the sun.
But I prefer the face you bring back home,
The colors softened by the wearing day,
Much as the sky when drained reveals the moon.

A CASE OF IDENTIFICATION

This is you photographed in '24,
Just about fifty years before your birth:
A lone female, still unidentified,
Posed with a group of seven surrealists.
(Some scholars argue the interior
Might be *Café Voltaire*, but are not sure.)

My case is really quite a simple one –
Not that this woman's wearing your beret,
Or that her lips are sensual yet thin,
Or that her eyes stare into mine as yours
Did when I told you that you seemed mature,
And not because she grins your telltale grin.

I rest my case completely on rapport:
No detail that a magnifying glass
Would let an avid student firmly note,
Simply the sudden, overwhelming sense
Of a rapport between her and Soupault,
The man whose eyes I use to see your picture.

AN EPISTLE FROM BARNABUS

From Barnabus to James and all the saints
Assembled in Jerusalem through love:
I find my faith is strong despite my doubts.
Indeed, I find my doubts a saving grace:
Without them I'd begin the journey home.
It takes a merry heart to travel here
And preach the word among barbarians.
Paul's faith is weaker, so he dare not doubt,
Or giggle at the folly of the work.
He's tireless in preaching to the nations
And would, I dare say, die if no conversions
Resulted from his lengthy exhortations.
Today he bored a little flock until
They would agree to anything at all
If doing so would merely silence him.
Good country folk, blessed with both charm and health,
They started strewing petals in our path,
Proclaimed me Jupiter incarnate and
Poor Paul my herald, winged Mercury.
He soon denounced them as idolaters
And put the fire on their altar out,
Though I laughed heartily, by Jupiter!
Pray for us both and, more, for all the world:
It has grown dark since our dear master's death.

TU FU REPLIES TO A QUERY ABOUT LI PO
in memory of Martin Seymour-Smith, 1928-1998

The commentators argue that his 'moon'
Does not mean *the* moon but instead 'the source
Of all enlightenment.' And drunkenness
Has nothing, after all, to do with wine
But with a 'spiritual ecstasy'.
The river is no river but 'the Way'.
Phooey! He was a mad old man, exiled,
With too few teeth left in his head, who loved
A woman he nicknamed the moon. (She had
The good sense to be unattainable.)
One night he had too much to drink and fell
Out of his boat, trying to embrace the moon –
Or rather her reflection in the water.
Women who dressed his bloated corpse report
His face took on a peaceful smile in death.
They say the moon waits for him by the pier,
A willow whose long hair touches the river.

THE CONDITION

Some speak of it in terms of their salvation.
It is no time or place but the condition
Of reckoning with love beyond all reason:
You are the months that make up my fifth season.

THE MASTER'S ROUTINE

You know the story anyway. Can see
It all. The long and empty platform where
The stationmaster in a peaked red cap
Rehearses how he would rush out to greet
The august persons he might someday welcome.
He paces briskly down the platform's length,
Comes to attention, clicks his heels, and bows.
A village girl, hiding and watching, laughs.
Arrival of the Emperor himself
Could never please him half so much as does
The sound of laughter that girl daily makes.

THINGS CHANGE

At first it was the obvious. The moon.
A slender birch reflected in the river.
Lovely, of course. That quiver in the air.
And yet you wanted more, demanded justice,
And so the obvious blessed with surprise:
A red-winged blackbird startled into flight.
Glorious. Glorious. Yet somehow insufficient
Until you suddenly became a Ford,
A black '51 Ford with dual exhausts
And foam dice dangling from the rearview mirror.
Sweet Christ, no chance now. So I saw you in
The massive bell near Independence Hall.
No, not the bell, and not the crack in it,
Rather the force that gave that crack its birth.
Exquisite. Everything. When you became
The Philadelphia skyline from Route 3,
I gave up all hope of recovery.

IT'S TIME
for Michele Mollo

It's time for me to live on what I have,
The only thing I couldn't sell or give
Away, the only thing no one else wanted:
The chatter of the dead to which I've listened
With more attention than I've paid to life.

FIRST LIGHT

The maple sapling, planted near the drive,
Produced a mass of tiny leaves this year,
Providing camouflage that hides the bird
Who sits there singing long before the dawn
But then falls silent once first light appears.

CORPORATE HISTORY

The oddest things can break your heart. Through work,
I met a man who helped his former boss
To write a book, a history of the firm
That ten years earlier had let them go.
On each sheet where the man had made some change,
The old executive, in ballpoint pen,
Wrote out 'Approved' and then initialed it.

THE THIRD ASPECT

The Phoebe and Miss Abbey sides of you
Make conversation slightly difficult
Although more interesting than usual.

The wine glass drained, the face flushed, your white paws
Strike at me playfully; and the small teeth
Display your willingness to laugh or bite.

Back home, once the domesticated cat
Decides to settle in, no matter what
I say, you simply curl up on your spot.

The third aspect is what defines you most:
Phoebe at play, Miss Abbey fast asleep,
Their coal-black mistress with her moons for eyes

Crosses the throw rug and the wooden floor
The way her ancestress once padded through
A pyramid slaves built to house dead kings.

MOVING IN

The tent was up but still unoccupied
When I moved into it. I put the cot
Down at the far end of the concrete slab,
And made it up with clean, fresh-smelling sheets,
And shrouded it with a mosquito net.
I slid a clip into the M-16
And pulled a single round up to the chamber,
But then made sure I had the safety on.
My duffle bag had made itself at home,
Leaning against the cot down at the feet
Or, rather, where in time my feet would be.
I sat down then and smoked a cigarette,
Dead tired and yet afraid to go to sleep.

THE WAY

This is the way my best days end these days:
A cup of coffee and a cigarette
And the moist earpiece of the phone held close
So I can hear your low voice say goodnight.

A CONCLUSION

He stands beside her front steps in the rain,
Knocks on the door and waits. She opens it
A crack, looks out and asks, 'What do you want?'
He looks up at her, rain thick on his face,
And in reply asks her, 'What do you think?'
She opens the door wide then, with no words,
And he climbs up the steps and goes inside.

DEEP SLEEP

1
A Mystery

They say the Lord works in mysterious ways;
And so the coma lasted for nine days.

2
Two of a Kind

My raked and spotted hands remind me of
The hands of someone I once loved who died.

3
Disagreeable

The doctors seem unable to agree
On which of several problems is the worst:
Aortic tear; blood clot above the knee;
Unwillingness to breathe; or constant thirst.

4
A Stranger

I have been home, now, from the hospital
For seven months – no, it is almost eight –
And yet I sometimes think I am there still,
And that a stranger eats meals from my plate.

5
Cured

The foul-mouthed goat who smoked and drank too much
Came back without a vice but on a crutch.

6
Homesick

Moving among the living once again,
I start to miss the place where I had been.

THE PROMISE

If you put empty milk bottles with notes
In them on your front step last thing at night,
You will assure yourself a night of peace
And wake to find those empty bottles full.

THE NEW YEAR'S GIFT

Because we meet so rarely now,
The next time I knock on your door
You should answer wearing nothing
But the earrings that I gave you –
Blue topazes and amethysts
Suspended on two silver threads
With your hair tucked behind your ears
To show the pride you take in them.

ON A BEACH

The maple, an umbrella on a beach
Of grass, provides a little pool of shade
In which a robin lands to take a bath
And then stands in the sun until he dries.

AT DAWN

There is no use apportioning the blame
Or booking passage for the Hebrides:
Just shake your head, acknowledging she came
As deer at dawn emerge from stands of trees,
And her return was bound to be the same.

GENERAL GIAP IN 2006

His masters trot him out, a souvenir
With nothing now to either say or do,
But with a grin that spreads from ear to ear
When foreign voices speak of Dien Bien Phu.

POINT OF NO RETURN

I look in your direction but then learn
I lack the power to make my eyes return.

YARD WORK
in memory of Tom Bostelle, 1921-2005

One of the maple's broken limbs
Points to the shadows of its leaves
The way an arm gestures toward
The shadows of its strands of hair

As if the moving shadows there
Spell something other than a word –
The evidence of rolled-up sleeves
Or of a passing schoolboy's whims.

EXPRESS

You wake to hear a train and wonder if
It was the passing train that woke you up
Or something else that, by coincidence,
Permitted you to hear the distant train
That keeps you now from going back to sleep.

GARLANDS

At the beginning of the last century
Children in East Bengal were taught to sew
Garlands consisting of three kinds of flowers:
Jasmine; the Flower of Sadness; and Bakul.
Piercing these fragile blossoms with their needles
To carefully sew them into intricate patterns,
The children, once their labors were complete,
Could briefly wear the garlands around their necks.
Soon drunk with the aroma of the flowers,
They were obliged to tear the garlands off,
Throw them to the ground, and then stamp on them.
Petals from those flowers would reappear
From time to time through the entire summer,
Recalling both luxuriance and loss.

A LACQUERED FAN

After a cold and drenching rain, the sun
Opens the maple like a lacquered fan
A lady uses to flash messages
Across the Great Hall to the Emperor.

TRANSLATIONS

Finding Seattle weather in
An ancient Chinese poem
Translated by Arthur Waley
Made Weldon Kees wonder whether
Waley were still alive.

DRUTHERS

When you ask me about my travel plans
I tell you that, if I could have my druthers,
I'd fly by British Air to London's Heathrow,
Then take the special train to Paddington
And go by rail from there to Penzance, Cornwall.

After a single night spent at the Abbey
For luck, perhaps, or else for old times' sake,
I'll fly by chopper to the Scilly Isles,
There to admire for, say, eternity,
The way rock in old age resists the sea.

WAKING

On waking you find you recall the dream
In which you stand in sunlight near a wall
And see the shadow of your left hand rise
To shoo away the shadow of a bee.

INCONSIDERABLE

Sighing or saying, singing, groan or moan,
The variations on the theme of air
Manipulated by thought's interventions
Can, in the mass, seem inconsiderable;
Yet one word spoken by an individual,
What I lack when I have no word from you,
Reminds us that the air holds earth in place.

NEW POEMS

OLD SNAPSHOT OF OFFICE LIFE

Torn bits of paper rolled up into balls
Litter the desk behind which you still sprawl,
The fingers of your right hand to your head
As if their touch could take away the pain.

And yet there's the beginning of a laugh,
The sly, slow generous spreading of full lips
That must be in response to what I said:
I wish my words could make you laugh again.

REFLECTIONS ON A CORNISH FAIRY TALE

Although the Marxists say that Jack's reward –
Marrying the boss's daughter as it were –
Is no more than a bourgeois dream come true
Transplanted to a quasi-feudal age,
I see it from another point of view.

Jack was not only poor and all alone,
But also small and young, and so quite weak,
With little but his cleverness to use
Against the giants who would terrorize –
Not Jack, of course – but his community.

Who were these giants, thundering around,
Stealing and killing, laying waste at will,
But bullies in a schoolyard, dictators,
The impulses at best called anti-social?
By contrast, Jack's instincts were clearly sound.

Wealth and the girl are what the hero gets
In Jack's case not because he wanted them
Especially or plotted their attainment,
But just because by slaying childish giants
He earned what most of us want out of life.

A FRIEND OF CAMUS REMEMBERS

It struck me funny then, not ominous,
Though now it seems to me an allegory.
She was the last and unlike all the others.
She was no student of philosophy
Or of art history. She was no actress
Or someone who made sculptures out of junk.
I do not think she even read his books
And wonder now whether she knew he wrote.

She was a tough girl from a tough neighborhood
Who had no wish to get to know his friends
Or share his social life in any way.
Wearing a leather jacket in the doorway
Of the Café de Flore, she paced impatiently
Until he slipped away apologetically
And, with his arm gentle around her waist,
They turned to disappear into the night.

THE SPY WHO STAYED OUT IN THE COLD

Once Leamas saw that both sides were the same,
He knew he'd rather die than play their game:
'Jump, Alec, jump!' he heard George Smiley call,
But turned away and climbed back down the wall.

TWO HORSES

> In the summer of 1788, a man speaks to a table of drinkers in the garden behind Philadelphia's City Tavern

I was a boy, just an apprentice then
When we left Valley Forge and marched to Monmouth.
Lucky, I was – in the artillery,
Serving with Colonel Eleazer Oswald.
A printer he is now right down the street
In Black Horse Lane – the publisher, in fact,
Of *The Independent Gazeteer*
Where ink is spilled for our new government.
He made a valiant officer but proud
And when he was passed over after Monmouth
He suddenly resigned and fought no more.
'Achilles in his tent,' they called him then,
The sorry wits of Philadelphia.
At Monmouth, though, the Colonel served with honor
And certainly deserved promotion too.
Washington should have intervened but claimed
Chaos would reign if he allowed himself
To override decisions others made
Simply because he disagreed with them.
He had a point, you know, but Colonel Oswald ...

Early the day took shape as a disaster
Largely because of General Lee, of course.
Some now say General Lee was treacherous,
Serving the British in our uniform;
Others claim that he was incompetent
And thus unfit to hold a field command.
I say he lacked the heart, the taste for killing

Much less the taste for maybe being killed.
Remember he refused command at first
But then demanded it once it was placed
In other hands. The stink of politics
In that, I say, a fear that someone else
Might benefit because of his refusal.
When he fled from the British before noon
I bet he wished, by Christ, he had refused.

Our purpose was to slow the British down
As they evacuated to New York,
Just slow them down until our major force
That Washington would lead could reach the spot
And so engage the enemy in strength.
Our fleeing from the field destroyed that plan,
But once the red coats followed us they drew
Closer to forces gathered in our rear.
Washington took over Lee's command and placed
Him under arrest, was heard to swear an oath,
And rode like mad to turn our troops around,
Waving his sword and screaming like a demon.
He somehow gave me strength to wheel my gun
And push it with no cart back up the hill
To send balls flying at the British ranks.
We fought the way we never fought before
And little stays in mind now but a blur,
Smoke in the nostrils, and the awful noise.
What I remember most now is the eye
Of a white stallion, fallen near a ditch,
That Washington had ridden to its death,
Rode it until its mighty heart gave out,
And then, through smoke, the sight of Washington

Charging again, but on a chestnut mare.
I thought then that he must be a magician,
Conjuring horses from the empty ground,
So is it any wonder some folk say
They willingly would make him our first king?

THE FIRST LADY'S INITIATIVE

Melania makes the president repeat,
'I must not cyberbully when I tweet.'

ON THE COUNTRY ESTATE OF JULIUS MARTIALIS
Translated with Robert F. Boughner (1946-2017) from the Latin of Martial's Epigram IV.64

Those few acres of Julius Martialis,
More fortunate than the garden of the Hesperides,
Lie on the ridge of the Janiculum.
The hills form wide retreats that lead toward
The summit where a slightly arched plateau
Takes pleasure in a calm and lovely sky,
And when fog forms a roof above curved valleys
It seems to glow with its own special light.
The angled peaks that top the lofty house
Slowly reach up to move toward the stars.
From here the view is of the Lordly Hills
And all the wealth and grandeur Rome contains,
The Alban Hills, and those above Tusculum,
The coolness caught below the city there,
The villages of Fidenae and Redstone,
As well as that site flushed with Virgin's blood –
The flourishing grove sacred to Anna Perenna.
Drivers on the Flaminian and Salarian Ways
From here are visible but wagon wheels
Emit no sound to break a pleasant sleep
Just as no sailor's cries or noises from
The Tiber with its shipping reach this place
Despite its closeness to the Mulvian Bridge.
The master makes this countryside estate
So welcome that it must be called a home.
The host extends such hospitality,
In so polite a way and generous,
So undemanding, that his guests are bound

To come to think of this place as their own.
You will become convinced the household gods
Here must be those of dutiful Alcinous,
The host who heard Ulysses tell his tale,
Or those of Molorchus, the farmer who
Showed hospitality to Hercules
And so received a generous reward.
These things might not seem much to those who farm
In frozen Tivoli or Palestrina,
Worked by the swinging of a hundred hoes,
Or those with ornate mansions up in Sezze,
And yet to me those places are as nothing
When held up in comparison with these
Few acres owned by Julius Martialis.

A PICTURE OF JEROME

This painting from the fourteenth century,
Made by an unknown hand, yet personal –
Images from a dream perhaps, at least
The work of someone who convinced himself
A lack of realism was the way to truth,
Someone given to paradoxes, I guess,
Who sought out life abundant as a hermit.

I think he must have been a Roman – an
Aristocrat who saw the Manger once
In Santa Maria Maggiore
Bathed in sunlight and somehow felt compelled
To follow Saint Jerome to Bethlehem,
Thinking in exile he would find a home.
A natural gift combined with training gained
Among Venetian masters meant that he
Could execute the vision when it came.

The furniture of the scriptorium –
The wooden bench, the stand holding a book –
Have been placed here, outdoors and in a desert,
A desert not of sand but made of rock:
Sheer cliffs of granite forming seven peaks,
A tribute to the seven Hills of Rome,
Ring both the furniture and the Saint himself.
Jerome sits in a scarlet hat and cloak
Holding a pen in his left hand to write
On what appears to be a parchment scroll.

A single building sits beyond the mountains,
The place where the scriptorium belongs,
The monastery where our Roman lives
Devoted to the memory of Jerome.
Beside the seated Saint, just to his right,
A lion, tame, and with a crooked smile,
Lifts his front paws in homage to the Saint,
Suggesting that he translates words by Mark.

And yet the oddest image of them all
Is a small scrawny tree that springs from rock,
A curved stick with a covering of leaves,
Placed at the high point of the picture, up
Above the Saint's head in a golden sky.
Although unjustified, I have to think
This little tree points to eternal life,
The paradox and wisdom of the whole:
Whoever made this picture seems to mean
Jerome says far more now than when he lived.

A PORTRAIT FROM THE LIFE

Critics are bound to say the thing is slight,
A sketch and little more of just a head;
Sitter and painter both unknown, but quite
Clearly a pair of lovers now long dead.
Such data – hunches – should not influence
Our judgment of a work: it is technique
Or else the tracking of a provenance
That lets us sort the strong work from the weak.

She looks up at the painter with a stare
As he adjusts the oak-wreath in her hair
That I find suddenly familiar
And so begin confusing you with her –
Recognizing the earrings that she wears
As those I first saw dangling from your ears.

A CELEBRATION

I woke up early Easter Sunday morning,
Showered and shaved, and dressed up in a suit –
The tan poplin that symbolizes spring –
And put on my new tie, the floral print
I ordered from J. Press online, and so
They sent it to me safely through the mail.
I went downstairs and put on my straw hat,
A pork pie with a feather in its band,
Then went outside and looked up at the sun
And walked to Merwood Park to celebrate
The resurrection despite the world's pandemic
By sitting on a bench beside the creek.